CATCH THE SPIRIT, BELOVED!

from clinical depression toward wellness

Roberta Thomas Smith

Catch the Spirit, Beloved!
From Clinical Depression toward Wellness

Published by CampCrest Publishing,
Hidden Hollow Lane, Chickamauga, Georgia

ISBN 13: 978-0-578-77164-9

First Printing—September 2020

COVER ILLUSTRATION BY WILLIAM HAMLET SMITH

Cover designed by Noah Craig, Dunlap, Tennessee
Editing, interior design, and typesetting by Rick Steele Editorial Services
(https://steeleeditorialservices.myportfolio.com)

Printed in the United States of America

acknowledgments

My utmost gratitude for the abundance of kindness, patience, and overwhelming assistance given me by my dear niece, Sally Jean Thomas Worland, and her dear husband, David Mel Worland, in having this collection of writings become published.

introduction

Over a period of years, these writings were gathered as I battled a clinical depression that was treated with various methods (including electro-convulsive shock therapy). The entries progress through a dark maze to a change of focus. Hopefully, this reflects the title—CATCH THE SPIRIT, BELOVED!

That is my reason for believing the collection may have significance for other readers. They show a progression from illness to wellness . . . from hospitalizations to loss of family . . . to divorce . . . to the climb at working at a job . . . to recertifying a teacher's certificate in three states . . . to teaching, again, for thirteen years. One of the most important parts of my healing was reconciling with and remarrying my former husband.

words to begin

The poem "PATHS" by my dear friend, Anne Hughes, reveals what life may bring and, in the last verse, what we need to bring to life. On my life's path, I'll vow that these two perspectives are valid, indeed.

I see parallels in the sequence of this poem's ideas and my entering into and coming out of a clinical depression that consumed more than ten years. The parallel shows my thoughts evolving into a spirit...the chronicle of which I offer for your reading—CATCH THE SPIRIT, BELOVED!

Thank you, Anne, for this poem. It has inspired me and helped...as has your friendship, to rekindle faith to continue the journeying with (as you penned) "fresh courage."

Many significant people have helped and continue to help in that regard. My desire to not omit a single name keeps me from listing. A list would begin with my mother and father and include all the persons with whom I have had the privilege to cross paths... most especially my husband and our children. My vocabulary doesn't begin to provide me words to describe the oceans of feelings and love there. I began too late in life to realize that there is something to learn from each person we know, even from those with whom we may not have had pleasant relationships. At times, the unpleasantness remembered brings pained memories, but while not forgetting, my learning to struggle to forgive (myself as much as others) will bring a peaceful reward, I trust.

The realization of each gift from each individual may come only after much time passes. Nothing, though, is ever wasted if we look for the gift and the good of a person.

"Paths" by Anne Godwin Hughes appears on the following page.

PATHS

Our lives have many lanes
down which we must walk...
And as we walk, we encounter
paths of different views–
Some are sad and troubled.
They harbor anxious and trying hours.
Others are filled with warmth
and good cheer.
They are flooded with sunlight –
bright and still.

Heartaches come and go–a time
of tears and pain–
There are times we walk
with aching hearts
Through a desolate land–
And the burden of regret makes
us ever so weary.
The turmoil of our soul's labor
heavily upon us, and hold us prisoner.

But we must free our (own) souls
Let them flow with the billowing wind
Flying free with silent force...
Riding the rushing white clouds
high against the sky.
We'll greet each dawning with
tender and knowing eyes...
Confident in the fresh courage
so keenly felt.

By Anne Godwin Hughes

CATCH THE SPIRIT, BELOVED!

The date after the selection reflects the date journaled, not necessarily the date first noted or composed, though in some instances, the two would be the same.

"So, the religious life, after all, is not a matter of trying to reach the bottom of things to satisfy one's intellectual curiosity. It is an intensely practical matter. So, as a matter of fact, I know that they who serve God grow in blessedness and peace and usefulness; those who accept Christ have not only a guide, but a motive power...a real inward treasure of thought, of hope, of content. For them there is light ahead and a path, and their minds dwell richly on things eternal.

"The church has always been the environment in which this belief and faith in God and Christ have been emphasized, enforced, and nurtured."

From *The Episcopal Church* by George Parker Atwater
July, 1976

Happy Rockefeller quotes Edith Hamilton from a book sent to Happy by Robert Kennedy. Edith Hamilton observed, "Civilization is the art of compromise."

Happy states, "Otherwise you would never go beyond the social development of children who try to solve everything by fighting."

July 1976

"One of my most profound experiences arose because of a mule they gave me to plow furrows for tobacco planting. I was feeling pretty much alone that summer, as my stepmother had died the winter before, so the mule became my closest friend. It was just an ordinary mule, but it was very patient while I hitched it to the plow. Every morning before hitching it, I'd go to the corn crib, shuck an ear, and feed the animal. Pretty soon, it began to anticipate this little treat and would be waiting for me with its head over the pasture fence.

"In the fall, when I returned to the farm for a weekend, I found my mule was gone. That morning at breakfast I asked my friend's father what happened to it. He gave me a big snort. 'Durn you, boy. You ruined that mule! We couldn't get a lick of work out of it after you left.'

"I never had the courage to ask the next obvious question. I suppose I knew that I had caused its death. It wasn't until years later that I unscrambled that unpleasant morning in my mind and exonerated myself of the blame. It was man's inhumanity all over again. Such a simple reward would have guaranteed that farmer the best mule on the place. Just a little act of kindness . . . an ear of corn to start the day."

From *Images of Yesterday* by Art Gore
July 1976

CATCH THE SPIRIT, BELOVED!

Though I can't recall the exact quote, I recall reading that the greatest realization one can have is his personal obligation or commitment to God. This is not exactly the quote, but it seems the essence of these words is so important. The meaning seems to become clearer to me as time goes by.

R. T. S.
July 1976

Though it is giving, not receiving, that gives meaning to life . . . at times, receiving graciously, *is* the most giving.

R. T. S.
August 1976

"What distinguishes the 'elite' from the masses is only their insistence upon quality. This implies a responsibility to all for all, to the past for the future, which is the reflection of a humble and spontaneous response to life . . . with its endless possibilities, and its unique present, which never happens twice."

From *Markings* by Dag Hammarskjold
August 1976

"I'll say this for death: It sure as hell teaches one a lot about living. One comes to have an exquisite appreciation of a personal history dotted with failures . . . of integrity ignored, of procrastination, of vulnerability to obligation and custom, to public and private applause. It is in facing death that one understands that transcending one's own limitations and those imposed by fate, is possible only through the exercise of choice: in the dying, the choice of how one meets the pain, the loneliness, the fear; in the living, choosing to sustain and integrate new, more deeply satisfying structures consistent with a value system conceived against the ferment of crisis. This restructuring requires a sharp memory for the hundreds of internal dialogues that took place, for the chidings, for the bargains struck with death or God or even one's own soul."

* *

"The major part of this change for me was change of focus: from things to people, from intellect to emotions, from form to process, from uncertainty to conviction. You do what you have to do. Concern that this could make a hedonist of one presumes that a new set of values would be entirely self-serving in the narrowest sense; it ignores the impact of love and human intercourse, of intimacy and transcendence. If anything, the crisis I experienced plunges me more deeply into a commitment to life and living. It is here where all that we live for, all that we search for resides . . . in that indefinable something that pulls a small person out of herself and shoves her up face to face with the firmament, eyeball to eyeball with her own reflection in the starry night, and the furious sun, the limitless reaches of intellect, imagination, and spirit."

From the article "I'll Say This For Death" by Stephanie Cook. Stephanie, at 36, writes of how facing death as a cancer patient brought her to a new reality of life.

August 1976

CATCH THE SPIRIT, BELOVED!

"In times of adversity, it's extremely comforting to have true friends."

From a letter of the Reverend D. S. MacDonald, Principal of
St. Mark's Episcopal School, Ft. Lauderdale, FL
August 1976

The ones in life who are sad are not sad because they have nothing about which to be joyous; nor are the ones who are joyous, joyous because they have nothing about which to be sad.

R. T. S.
August 1976

"We sometimes see only that which we want to see...so much so, that we often see that which isn't even there."

Eric Hoffer, longshoreman and philosopher
September 1976

When feelings drain, alone I sit
to contemplate.
To put in order, bit by bit
the transpired fate.
Again, it's changing feelings
still, that give me hope.
Again, it's changing feelings
still, that make me grope.
The mind must come to settle
soon on some true hold.
Undecided and unsure lead
to sad states, I'm told.
To be perplexed is not God's plan.
Of this I'm sure.
That's man's inhumanness to man.
Design your cure.
Accept the way of prayer for peace
as St. Francis prayed.
Giving should make a sure
release for feelings strayed.

R. T. S.
September 1976

CATCH THE SPIRIT, BELOVED!

Yes! There's order in the plan of things.
There's order in the stars.
Yes! There's order in the universe.
O God! What glorious bars.
To see the order day to day is such
a splendid gift.
God gives it, oh so freely, to those
who seek the lift.

R. T. S.
September 1976

Congressman Ron Paul (R. Texas) has good words . . . No, rather more than mere good words for West Point's honor code. "Why should the military academies cling to such an 'outmoded' code of student ethics? There is one very good reason why they do and should: The concept of personal honor is basic to the west's military tradition. The whole idea of an honor code is essentially military or even feudal . . . a tradition as old as the early middle ages in Europe. It is probably true, as sociologist, Robert Nisbet, has remarked, that in American institutions of higher education, only in the military academies and a handful of colleges in the south could a student honor code be maintained successfully. The south is still influenced by cultural remnants that are basically the product of a military code. (The southern tradition values personal loyalty more than profit, the family name more than family income, a man's word more than forms in triplicate.) This is a gentleman's code....Every student who applies (to West Point) through my office should know in advance that I support the code."

from *National Review Magazine*
September 1976

The Lord is my light
And my salvation;
Whom shall I fear?
The Lord is the strength
of my life;
Of whom shall I be afraid?

Psalm 27:1
October 1976

"Catch the spirit, beloved!"

From Bishop James Duncan's sermon at the 1976 Diocesan Convention at Key Biscayne, FL

October 29, 1976

Talent is built in solitude, but character is formed in the stream of life.

From a reading selection,
the source of which I don't recall.

October 1976

St. Thomas says that, "There is in man a certain inclination to the good, corresponding to his rational nature: And this inclination is proper to man alone. So man has a natural inclination to know the truth about God and to live in society. In this respect there come under the natural law all actions connected with such inclinations: namely, that a man should avoid ignorance, that he must not give offense to others with whom he must associate and all actions of a like nature." As usual, St. Thomas has something like the answer.

Quote used in the book *Inveighing We Will Go,*
by William F. Buckley, Jr.

October, 1976

CATCH THE SPIRIT, BELOVED!

"Something of what I mean may be conveyed by an encounter with a parent at the close of a recent school day. With eyes bright and a broad smile, the mother, holding a child with each hand, passed me and stated enthusiastically, 'It's catching!'"

" 'What is?' I asked.

" 'The spirit,' she responded. 'It's tremendous!'"

From a report by the Reverend Douglas S. MacDonald, Principal, St. Mark's Episcopal School, Ft. Lauderdale, FL (commenting on the spirit at the school).

November, 1976

Preamble to the will of James Alexander Gray
Past President of R. J. Reynolds Tobacco Company
Winston-Salem, North Carolina

"I desire to testify and give thanks for the goodness of God, who has blessed me far beyond my merit; for the constant devotion of my wife, the steadfast loyalty of my family, the rich fellowship of my friends, the stalwart cooperation of those with whom I have associated in business, the strength for daily toil, the joy of living, the beauty of the world, the inexpressible reward of striving, even in a most imperfect way, to follow Christ, and the glorious certainty of life eternal and abundant. . . . These are my real possessions."

James A. Gray died in 1952.
November 1976

"If you don't believe I'm sinking . . . look what a hole I'm in. If you don't believe I love you . . . look what a fool I've been."

From a 19th century black poet
November 1976

DESIDERATA

Go placidly amid the noise and haste, and remember what peace there may be in silence.

As far as possible, without surrender, be on good terms with all persons.

Speak your truth quietly and clearly, and listen to others, even the dull and ignorant . . . they, too, have their story.

Avoid loud, aggressive persons; they are a vexation to the spirit.

If you compare yourself with others, you may become bitter and vain, for always there will be greater and lesser persons than yourself.

Enjoy your achievements as well as your plans.

Keep interested in your own career, however humble. It is a real possession in the changing fortunes of time.

Exercise caution in your business affairs, for the world is full of trickery; but let this not blind you to what virtue there is.

Many persons strive for high ideals, and everywhere life is full of heroism.

Be yourself. Especially do not feign affection.

Neither be cynical about love; for in the face of all aridity and disenchantment it is perennial as the grass.

Take kindly the counsel of the years, gracefully surrendering the things of youth.

Nurture strength of spirit to shield you in sudden misfortune, but do not distress yourself with imaginings.

Many fears are born of fatigue and loneliness.

Beyond a wholesome discipline, be gentle with yourself.

You are a child of the universe, no less than the trees and the stars; you have a right to be here.

And . . . whether or not it is clear to you, no doubt the universe is unfolding as it should.

Therefore be at peace with God, whatever you perceive Him to be.

And whatever your labors and aspirations, in the noisy confusion of life, keep peace with your soul.

With all its sham, drudgery, and broken dreams, it is still a beautiful world.

Be careful.

Strive to be happy.

Found in Old St. Paul's Church, Baltimore, MD, dated 1662

December 1976

CATCH THE SPIRIT, BELOVED!

"Lord, we long for peace, the peace of love, of understanding, of kindness, of gentleness. And if we live in the world at all, we often have to put up with something very different . . . with struggle, and hatred, with misunderstanding, coldness, harshness. We need your courage to see the working out of love, even when all seems dark around us."

Prayer in *Day By Day*, Episcopal tract issued monthly
January 1977

The only way to resolve uncertainty is to discover the seed of the kingdom working within us, and to notice that it has a life of its own. Given even a minimal chance it pushes out its shoots toward loving others and towards a simple reliance and trust that it will be permitted to grow.

Unknown source
January 1977

CATCH THE SPIRIT, BELOVED!

From emptiness, deliver me.
To have found and yet to
feel a loss.
This is so unfair of me.
God wants me to be joyful.
Why can't I shed this feeling of loss?
It should have been so fine.
Where is that elusive peace?
To have found and yet to feel a loss.
One must encounter one's own
contentedness.
It is within the soul...not
outside the mind.

R. T. S.
Spring, 1977

"We cannot afford to spend this short life on matters nonessential. Beware of spiritual compromise. A reduced Christ can never bring God's kingdom to pass. Don't look for the easiest Christian way. Look for the greatest Christian good, even if it costs you more.

* Magnify your Christian privilege.
* Exalt Christ.
* Be loyal to His church.
* Christ is your one master.
* Tolerate no other."

From the book *Faith and Practice* by Frank E. Williams
June, 1977

CATCH THE SPIRIT, BELOVED!

The struggle . . . the pain . . . the climb
to hold truth,
to not let go.
Then the soul, illumined once again
by the ecstasy of God!
Nothing that I am,
to feel such joy,
such hope, such love!
To think one ever had to ask
His way of truth.
His holding on
to the faltering soul
which needs love alone.
Needs to give and share love.
Nothing that I am,
to have the chance
to do God's will.
The pieces fall into place
to do his will.
Accept the call.
Simplicity is the key to unlock
the contrite heart, the maze of life.
Nothing that I am,
God is the all.
God is the love.

R. T. S.
July 1977

Hold on to love that carries through—
that love which has no end.
It magnifies and beautifies.
True glory it will send.
Please heart be still.
Hear God's sweet voice.
And calm and patient be.
For if the love which brought you here
is a true and holy one,
then joy will follow in the morn—
a joy surpassed by none.

R. T. S.
August 1977

CATCH THE SPIRIT, BELOVED!

Toward understanding–
Toward hope–
Toward searching–
Toward love–
Toward God–
Let my path, dear God.
I love–
I hope–
I search–
I seek to understand–
I seek God–
Seek me, dear Lord.

R. T. S.
September 1977

Hugh Latimer, famed English cleric, was once invited to speak before the king of England. That Sunday, preparing for the appearance, he said, "I heard an inner voice saying, 'Latimer, be careful what you say today, because you will speak before the king.' But after a while, I heard another voice saying, 'Latimer, be careful what you say today, because you will be speaking before the King of Kings.'"

In judgment, it is the verdict of the higher court that counts.

October 1977

CATCH THE SPIRIT, BELOVED!

A man and his son were leading a donkey to town. A passerby laughed at them for walking while the donkey had no load. So, the man had the boy ride. Before long, they met a man who took the boy to task for riding while his poor tired father walked. The boy got off. The man got on. Soon, another traveler called the man selfish because he was making the little boy walk. To neutralize this objection, they both got on the donkey only to be accused of cruelty to animals. In desperation, they tied the donkey's feet together, put a pole between them and began to carry the donkey. But the people laughed so much that they let the donkey down. As they did, the animal began to kick. He rolled into the river and drowned.

No need to state the moral.

From an Aesop fable, "On Trying to Please Others"
October 1977

*Two things upon this changing earth
can neither change nor end–
the splendor of Christ's humble birth,
the love of friend for friend.*

Unknown author
Christmas, 1977

"To attain to knowledge of truth demands far more effort than it takes to acquire practical and scientific learning. Neither the reading of a vast number of books, nor familiarity with the history of Christianity, nor the study of different theological systems can bring us to our goal, unless we continuously cling to the commandments of Christ."

From *His Life Is Mine* by Archimandrite Sophrony
February 1978

They also serve who only stand and wait.

From *On His Blindness,* by John Milton
February 1978

The steely gray of the
stormy sky–
The iron blue sweep of
clouds–
Soon rain will pelt us
with its thudding drops,
and cool water will
nourish nature's growth.

R. T. S.
July 1978
(In hospital)

To recognize the faults
within–
To recognize one's full
of sin–
To overcome will be the task,
and then in glory we shall bask.

R. T. S.
July 1978
(In hospital)

Isolation–
Desolation–
Somewhere, Some day
There will be consolation.

R. T. S.

Humor, recover, humor,
the main ingredient
for balance.

R. T. S.

From self, deliver me.
To be at peace with God–
My whole desire is towards
this aim.

R. T. S.
July 1978
(In hospital)

The city calls.
The lights . . . they beam.
My hope . . . it falls.
My broken dream. . . .
Through tinted glass
life still goes on.
Lord, help me pass
each day as song.

R. T. S.
July 1978
(In hospital)

CATCH THE SPIRIT, BELOVED!

"There are many people, who with a real desire to pray, never bring any spiritual reality to birth in their souls because they turn themselves from book to book, from teacher to teacher, losing themselves in a multitude of different forms of words, spending time in saying many prayers, but praying little. A restless hen that frequently leaves the nest to find a better site, or spends much of her time rearranging the eggs will never hatch chicks; for only a quiet and persistent brooding will enable the dormant life to develop to the birth. In meditation we seek devotion; in affective prayer we find, and yet have to persevere in knocking, so that if the Master of Life should of His will open the door of contemplative knowledge, we are waiting on the threshold."

From *A Pilgrim's Book of Prayers* by Gilbert Shaw
June 1979

"It does not follow, however, that we can do right just by making up our minds. Only God can rescue us from sin. We need to be forgiven; we need to pray; we need to receive Holy Communion. Some of us need more. There are habits that can be conquered only with the help of a doctor; there are habits that can be conquered only with the help of a priest. If we want them conquered we must use that help. If we fail because we did not use God's appointed means, we have only ourselves to thank."

From *God Came Down* by John S. Baldwin
July 1979

"And . . . while prayer is our surest way of helping others, it is also the safest way, in that no true prayer can bring harm to another soul.

" 'Say little about God to others and much about others to God,' is a wise rule (although there are times when we must speak to others of God if we would not be cowardly or cruel).

From *The Work of Prayer*, by James O. S. Huntington
July 1979

A PRAYER ON RISING

I praise my God this day:
I give myself to God this day:
I ask God to help me this day.

From *The Work of Prayer* by James O. S. Huntington
October 1979

"It would be wrong to dwell derisively on sincere strivings after truth. But, in all charity, the Christian must note the unhealthy aspect of any long-term policy of studying your way to God at the fireside by means of library books. We must deprecate the idea that God has been so unjust as to locate Himself at the end of a long course of academic study which you wouldn't be equal to if you failed your eleven plus or your college entrance examination, and which you wouldn't have time for if you contracted galloping consumption. It is dangerous to suggest that arrival at God's truth can be attained only after years of study needing a trained academic mind. God is not so unloving, so unjust as to have weighted faith in favor of the intellectuals. The spiritually robust man does not need to plow through even one volume of Gifford's lectures before he can confidently recite the Apostles' Creed."

From *The Christian Man* by Harry Blamires
January 1980

His strength that surrenders
to no willful ways,
His tenderness like a first kiss—
this one who has meant for me
happier days
has changed the pathway
toward bliss.
His earnestness, tolerance,
and steadfast resolve
has meant for so many new life.
To be just a part of that thread
that's evolved
makes it worth all the self-centered strife.
So,
My hope for the future
will be for new hope,
for the kind that can
bring one true rest.
An unlocking of heart
and soul . . . a temper
to cope.
He's given so much.
I'm so blessed.

R. T. S.
January 1982

CATCH THE SPIRIT, BELOVED!

Ye watchers and ye holy ones,
bright seraphs, cherubim and thrones,
raise the glad strain.
Alleluia!
Cry out dominions, princedoms, powers,
virtues, archangels, angels' choirs,
Alleluia, Alleluia, Alleluia, Alleluia
Alleluia!

Melody, Cologne, Gesangbuch, 1623
May 1982

Hopes dashed–
Resignation–
Acceptance of whatever comes.
Remain on this plane.
Such a fantasy,
you silly dreamer.

R. T. S.
May 1982

Though sadness seems the
only reality, take comfort
knowing that there is a
plan, a place, a hope, a
peace that will transcend
all our aching moments
here.

R. T. S.
May 1982

Before this day has ended,
let me voice this glad refrain.
For even this one wretched life,
our Jesus Christ was slain.

R. T. S.
May 1982

CATCH THE SPIRIT, BELOVED!

Gentle acceptance,
oh, quiet retreat
to full resignation
of now sure defeat.
But, if all is God's world,
then this will serve, too,
for some higher goals
than the ones I pursue.

R. T. S.
May 1982
(In hospital)

Frustration–
at what you are.
Emancipation–
from what you are.
Proclamation–
of what you are.
Restoration–
in what you are.
Condemnation–
to what you are.
Exoneration–
from what you are.
Adoration–
of the sweet God on high.

R. T. S.
May 1982

CATCH THE SPIRIT, BELOVED!

"For persons to cope with what they find in society and still live in love, they must have strength. If he finds no love, he can blame only the fact that he has no love. He must dedicate himself to love, be resolute in his love and unwavering in his love. He can depend upon no one or no thing for reinforcement and assurance but himself. This may be a lonely path. He should remember that: His main function is to help unfold his true Self; He must be able to forgive himself for being less than perfect: He must endeavor to love in order to be loved; He loves to love.

"To be a lover will require that you continually have the subtlety of the very wise, the flexibility of the child, the sensitivity of the artist, the understanding of the philosopher, the acceptance of the saint, the tolerance of the dedicated, the knowledge of the scholar, and the fortitude of the certain. A tall order! All these are already a part of his potential and will be realized through loving. It becomes a matter of loving your way to love."

Source unidentified
May 1982

"Father William Du Bay stated it far better than I, when he said, 'The most human thing we have to do in life is to learn to speak our honest convictions and feelings and live with the consequences. This is the first requirement of love, and it makes us vulnerable to other people who may ridicule us. But our vulnerability is the only thing we can give to other people.'"

From *Love* by Leo Buscaglia.
Dr. Buscaglia's basic theory is that love is learned and that everyone can and should learn to love.

May 1982

The way is long.
The road is hard.
We travel on.
We stay the guard.
Free up yourself
to all you know.
Let time go by.
You've yet to grow.

R. T. S.
May 1982

Erich Fromm has written, "To love means to commit oneself without guarantee, to give oneself completely in the hope that our love will produce love in the loved one. Love is an act of faith, and whatever is of little faith is also of little love."

From *Apprentices in Love* by Mark Gibbard
May 1982

The decision of faith is never final. It needs constant renewal in every fresh situation.

Rudolf Bultmann
May 1982

I know my Lord is near.
His words to me are dear.
He bids me rest,
consoles my heart,
and saves me from my fear.

R. T. S.

Praise God above,
My Lord and King.
He is my maker.
He has a purpose
for me here.
Be still, my doubtful heart.
Rest in God's love.

R. T. S.
May 1982

* *

This day we decided on divorce.
May 26, 1982

There was a time when days
would pass,
that I would play the fool.
But now I see that each day's time
is our Lord's lifetime school.

R. T. S.
May 1982

The mind seems dim.
My thoughts are few.
So uninspired
so sad and blue.
Wake spirit, please
and come within.
Surround me here.
Save me from sin.

R. T. S.
May 1982

CATCH THE SPIRIT, BELOVED!

There is a place of quiet rest, near to the heart of God.

From a hymn
May 1982

Comfort is such a pregnant word.
Its sound is like the sea,
the lulling of an ocean breeze,
the whisper of wind in a tall pine tree.
Its meaning has for everyone
a very special place; a time,
a friend, or even a dream,
or the memory of your face.
That face that conjures a million dreams
of how it might have been.
Yes . . . you, my love, are comfort to me,
my prayer song at each day's end.

R. T. S.
June 1982

"In incidentals, let us have diversity: In essentials, let us have unity: But in all things, let us have charity."

Pope John XXIII
July 1982

If ever there was a precious gift
in all the world to me,
It's got to be the time-tried words
of faith, hope, and charity.
To help us through each day and hour,
there's one which stands above.
Sweet charity is oh so dear,
because it stands for love.

R. T. S.
July 1982

CATCH THE SPIRIT, BELOVED!

Clouds suspended in the air,
billows and streaks are everywhere.
Shapes and forms go together to blend
a mural of nature's dividend.

R. T. S.
July 1982
(In hospital)

A friendly discussion is as stimulating as the sparks that fly when iron strikes iron.

Proverbs 27:17 (*The Living Bible*)
August 1982

When we recognize the hurt we've caused,
When we recognize the pain,
Where can we turn to right the wrong,
To cure our self-disdain?
The answer lies within our hearts
For God has put it there.
He grants us instant pardon,
If we come to Him in prayer.
We may not find a quickening cure,
Though it's been freely given.
But God will send us strength to bear
Our trials that lead toward heaven.

R. T. S.
August 1982

If heaven is beyond this earth,
Then what's this earth to me?
Is it where one begins a birth
Toward one's eternity?
Or, does it come some future day,
Or is it close at hand?
To me, I pose we truly say
Our glory is of this land.
To postpone 'til a later date
The time to see our God,
May mean that one was just too late.
One failed to see the prod.
The prod that comes in every act,
With every human action,
The nudge to joy—to not look back;
Today. . . . find satisfaction.
Heaven could begin on earth
If we but let it free.
This moment can complete the birth
Toward our eternity.

R. T. S.
August 1982

" 'I should not have believed in the Gospel,' said St. Augustine, 'unless the authority of the Catholic Church had moved me to it.' The Church is a school of faith, a home of love, a base for service, and a preparation for heaven. Christ loved the Church and gave Himself for it. So we are taught in Ephesians 5:22. 'What Christ loved enough to die for, I must love enough to live for.' "

From *I Believe and Why* by R. R. Williams, Bishop of Leicester
August 1982

The ebb and flow,
the to and fro,
the shoreline beach,
what can it teach?
The sinful pride
I long to hide,
even if I could,
t'would do no good.
Stay with today,
though you may sway.
As the tide comes in
you need to bend.
As it goes out
inside you shout,
I'll rest once more
just like the shore.
As the tide returns
your heart will yearn.
But let it know
it needs to grow.
You've made your bed.
A life of dread?
Then the blame is yours,
not life's tide-swept shores.

R. T. S.
October 1982

Addition:
So, with rising tide
let faith abide.
You will find life's glow
when you've learned to grow.

November 1982

Dear God above, hear my dim voice.
I love to say your name,
to reverence in its very sound,
and to all the world proclaim.
Proclaim the joy that you can bring,
though it is mixed with pain.
But one enhances the other more,
to remind us that he was slain.
Slain to show to all the world
the glory in that death.
With agony and ecstasy,
He drew His final breath.
Breath that gave the gift He gives
and brings us to our knees
to pray that we'll accept His call
to love as He would please.

R. T. S.
October 1982

The days have come and gone.
The mind has failed to learn.
Confusion—once again.
Will transcendence ever come?
So constant seems my love,
though fear becomes my foe,
and causes me to shrink,
when faith could help me grow.
Reminders of the past
creep in despite my will
to still the lonesome thoughts
to trudge and scathe life's hill.
The ever present woe
that causes my unrest
seems lack of trust and love
and shame, though it's confessed.
A spirit light and free
would seem to me a gift.
Trust God to fill my need
and furnish me the lift.

R. T. S.
November 1982

CATCH THE SPIRIT, BELOVED!

Continue in this path you trod,
and soon will come the day
when many things that you've held dear,
you'll see, have gone away.
Already gone are friends and folk
whom you hold dear this day.
They look at you and shake their heads.
They're sure you've lost your way.
But God always will be just one
who'll hold you in his heart.
He knows you're trying, though you fall
and stumble through the dark.
And some day there will come the time
when this world's deathly sway

will vanish . . . and you'll hope to see
revealed, the God of love you hope has
led your way.

R. T. S.
November 1982

Silence—the fullness of silence
Reflection—the quiet and peace
Abide in the stillness of silence
Transition—when all cares can cease.
The heart hears the voice of the Savior
illumined toward heaven-sent Grace.
All cares melt away to our Savior,
with longing to gaze at his face.

R. T. S.
November 1982

CATCH THE SPIRIT, BELOVED!

Once, there were three,
faith hope, and love
to help me through the day.
Until the faith began to slip,
but hope and love did stay.
As time went on
and hope grew dim
then finally passed away.
There still was love
to carry through
to help me through the day.
It has been said of these three words,
that the dearest one is love.
For without that to guide our acts,
there's no guidance from above.
But even though our aims are high
to make our acts of God.
Reflecting on my very own life
perhaps it's self that is the prod.
Perhaps if one can keep love's strength
by giving love away.
In time the two that I have lost
(faith and hope) will return…
I pray to stay.

R. T. S.
December 1982

ON ACCEPTING LOST LOVE

I've often heard, "Where there's life, there's hope."
I wonder if that's true.
Because it seems my heart will break to think
that I've lost you.
There are no words to fathom this,
the aching to the bone.
The helpless, hopeless trudging on,
the search to find a home.
So unwanted and alone
perhaps that isn't true. (Not if God is there.)
Nor am I just the only one,
for others feel this way, too.
But they have cause and have endured
much more than I could bear.
To think that I am so unique–
that certainly isn't fair.
So, if the phrase, "Where there's life, there's hope,"
can somehow be my guide,
perhaps I'll learn to follow through
and melt my foolish pride.

R. T. S.
December 1982

Lord, teach me to love.
Lord, teach me to pray.
Lord, teach me to share.
Lord, teach me to say
Thank you always, in my heart.
Thank you Lord for love.
Thank you Lord for prayer.
Thank you Lord for those who share.
Lord, thank you for the goodness in
the world, which is only one whisker
of a dandelion compared to your heaven's
glory and light!

R. T. S.
December 1982

"There must be an attempt to stay within the daily workings of life and to see that our goals cannot be set apart from the myriad incidents that make up a day's activities; inclusively our contact with the persons of the world.

"To feel set apart from such would tend to quicken the indulgence of self and lead further into the abyss of selfishness."

Source unidentified
January 1983

CATCH THE SPIRIT, BELOVED!

Never forget to remember the immensity of God, the vastness of His creation, the magnificence of His concern and His love for even the fallen sparrow; in the hope that one's perspective may be formed with an eye toward His service and His purpose . . . not one's own.

R. T. S.
January, 1983

Desiring,
Asking,
Accepting,
Loving,
Praising,
Rejoicing,
Celebrating,
God

R. T. S.
January 1983

Divorce granted, January 4, 1983.

Perseverance

January 1983

Question: What is our duty to our neighbor?

Answer: Our duty to our neighbor is to love them as ourselves and to do to other people as we wish them to do to us.

V. To love, honor, and help our parents and family; to honor those in authority, and to meet their just demands;

VI. To show respect for the life God has given us; to work and pray for peace; to bear no malice, prejudice, or hatred in our hearts; and to be kind to all the creatures of God;

VII. To use all our bodily desires as God intended;

VIII. To be honest and fair in our dealings; to seek justice, freedom, and the necessities of life for all people; and to use our talents and possessions as ones who must answer for them to God;

IX. To speak the truth, and not to mislead others by our silence;

X. To resist temptations to envy, greed, and jealousy; to rejoice in other people's gifts and graces; and to do our duty for the love of God, who has called us into fellowship with Him.

Book of Common Prayer, page 848 (Catechism)
January 1983

"It is as hard to see oneself as to look backwards without turning around."

Henry David Thoreau
January 1983

"What I ask for is absurd: that life shall have a meaning. What I strive for is impossible: that my life shall acquire a meaning."

Dag Hammarskjold
January 1983

"The purer the eye of her attention, the more power the soul finds within herself. But it is very rare to find a soul who is entirely free . . . whose purity is not soiled by the stain of some secret desire of her own. Strive, then, to constantly purify the eye of your attention until it becomes utterly simple and direct."

From *Markings* by Dag Hammarskjold
January 1983

CATCH THE SPIRIT, BELOVED!

"It has pleased God to make human communion a condition of communion with Him."

From *The Person Reborn* by Dr. Paul Tournier
January 1983

"We are not worth so much as to gather up the crumbs under thy table. But thou art the same Lord whose property is always to have mercy."

Book of Common Prayer, Rite I, Page 337

These words were so eloquently and gently delivered by the Reverend Mortimer Glover of St. James Episcopal Church in Wilmington, North Carolina. When I recall the newness of attendance of services in Episcopal churches at that time, it was his fervor in delivery of that particular passage that etched it on my mind.

Between 1983 and 1989

"Let the words of my mouth and the meditations of my heart be acceptable in thy sight, O Lord, my strength, and my redeemer."

Psalm 19:14

* *

"I know that my Redeemer liveth."

The above comment was uttered by William F. Buckley, Jr. in a magazine interview. The interviewer had asked Mr. Buckley if all dogma, at some point, does not dissipate or lose meaning (or words to that effect).

Mr. Buckley responded, "Not all, but some." Queried further as to why not all, he answered, "I know that my Redeemer liveth."

(This is a remembered quote many years after I first read it, so the wording may not be exact, but the idea conveyed, I believe, is everlasting.)

Between 1983 and 1989

My dearest Lord, if, in your infinite mercy, you could find it possible for me to have the chance to be able to share in my children's lives and to not feel so cut off from others, even though I know this lonely suffering is certainly no less than what I deserve for the kind of person I became, I pray that, somehow, once again, I could be near them and share, in the right way, your love in their lives . . . the good as well as the bad times and the strength to be of some help to them as they have been to me. I pray for the healing of my mind so that I could feel a shedding of the darkness that seems to hang inside my thoughts, keeping me from feeling free to express a concern and love for others.

R. T. S.
Between 1983 and 1989

CATCH THE SPIRIT, BELOVED!

For the peoples of the world . . . Peace

* *

"Make amends . . . endure . . . love"

The statement above was made by a patient of Dr. Paul Tournier's in his book, *Guilt and Grace*, after an intensive and long period of therapy. She had determined that this statement summed the discernment of wherein lay the answer as she continued her life.

* *

I believe there is a God.

R. T. S.
Between 1983 and 1989

I pray for those I love and for those who have come into my life that have taught me the beginnings of a total faith in Thee. These I love so fervently.

Lord, teach me how to love . . . how to follow your great commandments . . . not so others will love me, if that is your will, but so that I may be able to express your love by being what you want me to be.

Teach me, Lord, to lose concern for my own desires and wants, resting in the knowledge that you will provide for me, but also not shrinking from the responsibilities that you give me.

When one is given much, it behooves one to put aside pettiness and to avail ourselves continually, to the teachings of Jesus . . . seek out, I trust, the ones who can best interpret these teachings.

R. T. S.
Between 1983 and 1989

Why, dear God, does it seem that others take such pleasure in hurting me? Please, God, help me to live in your will this day. I wonder if it's because they think I have hurt others so much and deserve to have the same medicine over and over, so that I can never forget my wretchedness. It seems that I shall never forget it. I know I shan't. At times, it may *appear* that all matter of guilt is far from me.

R. T. S.
Between 1983 and 1989

Lord, to me, it seems there is no holy spirit in me, and that I have been quite presumptuous in naming this collection of writings thusly . . . if after all this time, I feel devoid of being able to relate my assurance that God has caring and loving concern for each individual. I feel my existence causes such a burden of duty to those in my family and to some that know me. I wish I knew how to show concern for their lives that didn't make them feel they must continue to say and/or do things to show me my lack of concern for others and also, my abounding selfishness, for this never seems to leave me, anyway.

Help me, dearest Lord, to someday be of some help in living the message that God, and only the love of God, can give us the assurance that there is a place for us in this world.

Help me, dearest Lord, to learn how to be a giver and a lover. Help me to want to do these things because God commands us to love, and that it is better to give than to receive . . . not because it promotes some feeling of satisfaction within myself.

Lord, tonight it seems to be my express and fervent desire to do whatever would be pleasing to you. Give me, I pray, the courage and the conviction to live in your will.

Help me, dearest Lord, to be able to have the will to relieve others of the tiresomeness of me and the repetition of my feeble attempts at gaining insight into how to live a Christian life.

Help me, dearest Lord, not to retreat to such a cloistered life, in the protection of my home, because our association with your people is the place for the purpose of Christianity, it would seem. If I'm not able to express your love in those associations, let me not be resentful or bitter and thus use the quiet time not always spent in selfish pursuits of the kingdom for myself, but prayerfully for the furthering of your kingdom in the lives of others.

With so many petitions for myself, dear Lord, let me close this prayer with thankfulness and praise to your holy name and a prayer for the further joyful spread of your kingdom tomorrow and each day after. In Jesus' name. Amen.

R. T. S.
between 1983 and 1989

CATCH THE SPIRIT, BELOVED!

PRAYER - GOD'S GIFT

"Prayer itself, as well as the answer to prayer, is a gift bestowed upon us not because we deserve it, but because we need it. And the worthfulness of prayer comes not from what we think or from what we feel, but from what the Holy Ghost does. By my prayers I do not move God to come to me, but God moves me to come to Him.

"The whole matter can be stated in a few words. There are certain things which God wants to give me, or wants to enable me to do towards Him. So, at the proper time, He sends His Holy Spirit to stir in me the desire for that which He has made ready for me to have or to do. If I welcome this desire then the Holy Ghost within my soul uses its powers, (mind, affection, will) to turn the desire into words and to make the words a prayer to God. The prayer value depends not upon the human spirit but upon the Divine Spirit. The prayer, therefore, is part of the gift. It is the channel which God, Himself, opens in a man's heart through which He may pour the blessing He purposes to bestow. Our prayers are not right prayers if they are not the work of the Divine Spirit within us, wanting what God wants."

* *

"So the very best and loudest prayer in the ear of God may come from a soul that feels itself bereft of His light and love, and yet for that very reason, longs all the more yearningly to be able to speak to Him. Let such a soul abandon itself to its mighty comrade and friend, the Holy Spirit. If it finds no other words, let it say, 'Lord, I believe, help thou mine unbelief. Lord, take my soul for I cannot make it Thine, and keep it for I cannot keep it Thine.'"

* *

"There is a recognition of His light and love and the need to continue to recognize that it is the desire of the Holy Spirit and not my desire that is of importance in fulfilling God's will.

"It is love that asks, that knocks, that finds, and that is faithful to what it finds."

Saint Augustine
between 1983 and 1989

"The only crescendo of significance that any of us ever make is the crescendo of the human heart."

Robert Shaw of the Robert Shaw Chorale
January 1992

"To laugh often and love much; to win the respect of intelligent persons and the affection of children; to earn the approbation of honest critics and endure the betrayal of false friends; to appreciate beauty; to find the best in others; to give of one's self; to leave the world a bit better, whether by a healthy child, a garden path, or a redeemed social condition; to have played and laughed with enthusiasm and sung with exaltation; to know even one life has breathed easier because you have lived . . . this is to have succeeded."

The above quote, shown to Gerald Ford, 38th President of the United States, reminded him of his parents, as being a credo by which they might have lived. He feels the definition would imply they indeed succeeded. Neither his friend, who showed him the quote, nor President Ford knew the author of the words. His father was his adoptive father, as his mother and his birth father divorced, and he had very little contact with him after that.

From *A Time to Heal* by Gerald Ford, pages 42–43
1996

President Jimmy Carter comments in his book, *Keeping Faith*, on the confusion and fragmentation with which our government has to function, causing him to feel it almost a miracle how well the nation survives and prospers. He thinks the answer lies in the bountiful blessings of our natural and financial resources, the wisdom of the forefathers who shaped our government and the inherent strength of our people. The focal points of political faith lie in either . . . the resilience of our diverse peoples, the wisdom of the Constitution and its derivative laws and customs, the national spirit of hope and confidence that has shaped our history, or the unchanging religious and moral principles that have always been there to guide America on its course. Sometimes, he says, we forget, and even deviate radically from our nation's historic path. But we soon remember the advantages of compassion for the weak, ethical standards, the beauty of our land, peace and human rights, the potential quality of our children's lives, and the strength we derive from one another as free people . . . unfettered except for self-imposed limits. Then . . . we are able to correct our mistakes, repair what we have damaged, and move on to better days.

From *Keeping Faith* by Jimmy Carter, pages 89–90
1998

President Ronald Reagan shares what he feels is the key to return America to a proper perspective on government. He is doing this in the context of visiting the Latin American countries and, specifically, in an address to Brazilian leaders in Sao Paul....

". . . the first principle to be embraced was that 'mankind will not be ruled,' in Thomas Jefferson's words, 'by a favored few.' The second is a pledge to every man, woman, and child: no matter what your background, no matter how low your station in life, there must be no limit on your ability to reach for the stars, to go as far as your God-given talents will take you. Trust the people; believe every human being is capable of greatness, capable of self-government . . . only when people are free to worship, create, and build, only when they are given a personal stake in deciding their destiny and benefiting from their own risks, only then do societies become dynamic, prosperous, progressive, and free."

From *An American Life* by Ronald Reagan, page 176
1998

WORDS TO BEGIN ... THE END ... OF THESE MUSINGS

Pages 100–102 are special to the height of specialness. They were written and read to our family by my husband on our first Christmas together after we remarried each other in August of that year. As he always did, in all of our life together, he gave the accolades, praise, and credit to others. His was a beautiful, wonderful, loving, generous spirit.

Page 103 is a letter from a fine priest/chaplain who responded when I asked for a copy of a particularly moving sermon he'd delivered.

Pages 104–108, the sermon, He'd baptized a baby that Sunday and fast-forwarded years ahead of the baptismal day to the year 2078. He spoke as if a letter had been received by the church from that baptized person, written on her 90th birthday. He read it to the congregation. In it she lovingly relates the many ways "the church" affected her life . . . for the better.

A CHRISTMAS CELEBRATION
AT SARAH'S

1998

As we gather here together and celebrate the birth of Christ, I am inspired by the power of our love, and being together as a family. I can't help but be hopeful by what I see and what I feel. Perhaps our lives always need to be in a stage of rebirth.

Recently Roberta sent me some notes from Dr. Stanley, the great preacher whom she enjoys listening to when she can, dealing with hopelessness. Dr. Stanley went on to say: "But, God made every human with hope, and that God is the cure for all hopelessness." Then after thinking further about the word "hope," it is clear that hope is the quality within our hearts which enables us to continue going. Hope can make each of us become a better person. I believe hope can dispel loneliness, and heartache, weariness and frustration. Then I read somewhere one time that there is no better nor blessed bondage than to be a prisoner of Hope. Now, let me refer back to the word "celebration," which I believe is one of the most exciting words I know. When defined, it may mean to perform a sacrament, to honor, to demonstrate satisfaction, by festivities, to observe a holiday, to observe a notable occasion. Thus, our meeting this weekend and being together is truly a celebration, and it is certainly a great privilege for me to be here with you, and I love you dearly, each and everyone.

So, my thoughts now run to this wonderful occasion of Christmas at Sarah's sweet home, a celebration of love, support, caring for each other. Perhaps no one family has more to celebrate and be thankful for. A poem I read a long time ago strikes me now:

He who only walks in sunshine misses all the joy of rain;
He who never suffers hardship, must forego it's healing pain.
To attain a perfect balance and a rich, full life to live,
there must be a careful blending of all things which life can give.

Each of you is a special work of God; no, we may not be free of imperfections, but who is in this world we live, but yet your hearts and your spirits are strong, as they can be, and let's be joyous and celebrate happily what we see.

There are four healthy people gathered in this room, loving one another, in a world of many blessings; able to see the beauty all around us, and hear each other talk and laugh; we can think, reason, decide, remember with the soundness of our minds, and we can walk and move about, and we all can really run, and can feel the sun, and all its brightness, and can touch and feel our senses; okay . . . these thoughts go on and on.

Then, let's pray and thank God for all we have; for Roberta, a wife, and mother, who dedicates her life to us all, who loves us when we sleep, and loves us when we fall. She is our champion and a saint of God, a lady of wisdom, a source of strength in our lives, and certainly, none can doubt her loveliness, commitment and love for Sarah, Michael, and me.

For Sarah, and the depth of her spirit; it's like that of a thoroughbred horse, running on down the track and never looking back, and that's probably why horses respect and like her.

She is living proof that all of us can achieve success and reach for newness in our lives, if we look forward to each new day, give it our very best. That's what Sarah is up to. We are very blessed to experience this great lady on this day, and may God always keep her in a very special way.

For Michael, and the renewal of his life. He is a prime example of a man in hot pursuit of a newly dedicated and directed path. His attitude, courage, and accomplishments are evidenced every day. So, God, we ask you to always keep him in your loving care, and we thank you for the inspiration of the life he shares with us.

Then, as for me, I ask you all to forgive me for seeming to worry so much, and regularly reflecting concern for my personal financial condition, lack of suitable income to retire and feel more comfortable about the future. Though all of this does bother me a bit, especially not having enough resources to help you all in a more meaningful way, I want you to know, I am really the wealthiest man on earth when I consider what a splendid and loving family I have.

So, as we celebrate this great day together, I raise my hand in salute, in respect, in honor to each and every one of you . . . I am truly touched by this day, and so very, very proud of this family. God bless you always and thank you for the joy you all bring to me, and may all your dreams come true. I love you very much. Merry Christmas, Happy New Year, and I ask God to keep you always free from harm, in good health and with peace of mind.

Bill/Dad
Bill/Dad

B.F.F.

Spring 1999

**Broward General
Medical Center**

1600 S. Andrews Avenue, Ft. Lauderdale, FL 33316 • (305) 355-4400
Wil Trower, Administrator

11/12/93

Dear Roberta,

Many thanks for your letter,
your check, and your kind
words.

The sermon on baptism
reflects the practical and very
meaningful ways that growing up
Christian can have for the
individual. It also reflects my
very deep belief that other people
are important in that process,
as well as the Almighty.

My best to you —

Sincerely,

Joe

A division of the North Broward Hospital District

Spring 1999

Mrs. Jonathan T. Jones
Los Angeles, California

November 9, 2078

To the Congregation of
All Saints' Episcopal Church
Fort Lauderdale, Florida

Dear Saints,

Today is my 90th birthday, and as a part of the celebration, I am taking the liberty of writing to you, even though you do not know who I am. My three children and their families are here celebrating with me, and we have had a wonderful time together. I am so grateful for their love. They share it with me and with many other people, and it never seems to run out.

I am rather feeble and confined to the house now. My eyesight has grown dim, but I can still read a little. Because I cannot write any more, due to arthritis, my grandson, John Patrick Jones, is writing as I dictate. He is such a fine young man, and he and his lovely wife have a beautiful little girl named Gregorie Pennewill Jones, after my mother's family. . . . I could go on and on talking about my wonderful family, but that is not the purpose of this letter. Actually, I find it difficult to pinpoint the reason for the letter—except that my heart is just so full of joy, and I want to share some of it with you. My life has been rich and full. O, so blessed! That is what I want you to know about.

The thing that prompted me to write this letter was my scrapbook. I had not looked at it in years—maybe twenty or more—but today we got it out to look at the pictures of me and the rest of the family. My grandchildren had never seen it. They have so enjoyed looking at all the collections of photographs and things. Among the many mementos in the book was a document certifying my baptism at All Saints' Church, Fort Lauderdale, on February 19, 1989, and the Sunday bulletin from that service. The children were so captivated by the knowledge that I had been born and baptized in Fort Lauderdale, Florida, and they wanted to know about the church, and the city and my early years there. Then, of course, they wanted to know about my life since then. So I told them. There was so much to tell, and as I talked, I realized that it was all related in some way to what took place at All Saints' Church almost ninety years ago. My whole life was stamped in a mysteriously splendid fashion by the beginning I had there. All Saints' is where I began my life as a Christian, marked, as they say, by God as his very own forever.

Of course I do not remember anything about the baptism, for I was only three months old. But I do remember hearing my mother and father speak about it. And my godparents—Lucie and Paula and John. They're all gone now, of course. But they were all so good to me and for me. I just loved it when they and my parents got together. Everyone had fun.

I can remember as a little tot going to church on Sundays. There was a lady named Susan who kept us in a big playroom while all the big people went to church. Then as I got older, we sometimes played in a bigger room, and sometimes outside on the swings. It was right next to the water. Sometimes I got frightened and sometimes I cried. But those people loved children, and most of the time I felt good being there.

I used to love to go there. The teachers at Sunday School were wonderful. I don't remember too many details, but my lasting impression is that it was a very happy time. You see, I was loved at All Saints' Church, just as I was loved at home. And those two places are where I learned how to love. I am so grateful that I had a chance to begin to learn that at a very early age. Grateful to my parents and godparents who did all they could to teach me that. And of course I am grateful to your parents and grandparents who, because they cared, nurtured me in the Christian Faith. They taught me and showed me at a child's level who Jesus is.

You know, it is interesting to try to remember your early child-hood. I found myself describing to my grandchildren some of the ministers I remember. There was one that my parents said had baptized me. I could not remember his name until I looked at the certificate. But I did remember that he had gray hair, and was very bald on the top, and had a kind of beaky nose, and that he seemed genuinely fond of me and my family.

One of the things very vivid in my mind is going to the Big Church with my family. I don't know how old I was, but I was so frightened by the bell. We were standing right under it one Sunday when it rang. We never got caught there again. But I remember being in church in those early years and that it was so difficult for me to be quiet and sit still. It seemed to upset my mother and father more than anyone else, really. My dad even pinched me one time. I knew what that meant.

Big Church was wonderful. Lots of choir people and acolytes processed in. The music seemed big and beautiful. When we sang, I joined in as best I could. There is where I learned about belonging to a family of people called the Church. Sometimes they would have the children come up front for a lesson or talk—like a little sermon. This was a family that loved God and worshiped Him and served Him. That family started me on the road of love. Then after church, we'd have juice and people laughed and talked and had a good time. And I felt good because I felt love, and because my mother and father were there, and they loved those people. It was a good time and I have pleasant memories.

I do not know what my life would have been like had I not been baptized. I suspect it would have been very different indeed, however. What began at All Saints' Church in 1989 continued throughout my growing-up years. Wherever we went to live, my parents always found a church home for us and the nurturing continued. Sometimes I was unaware of it. At other times I was very aware of it and rebelled and became difficult, especially during my college years. I almost never entered the church then. Still the faith was there, and I knew I belonged to God.

I suppose it was not until I married that I really went to church again—and then it was to the Presbyterian Church. My husband, Jonathan, was a pretty strong Presbyterian. I discovered, however, that though I'd been baptized in the Episcopal Church, it was not the Episcopal Church I joined. It was the whole Church, God's Church. And for the last sixty-five years, I have been as faithful to Jesus Christ as I could possibly be—as a member of the Presbyterian Church. But after all these years, I still miss the *Prayer Book* and the Episcopal service.

The important thing is that as a Christian I learned to cope with life. It has not all been easy. In fact, there were some quite difficult times. But because I was sure of God's love and forgiveness, I could face those times. Somewhere along the way, other Christians had taught me that I was okay. And so I learned to love myself. And this enabled me to love other people. Most of the time I even felt good about myself—in that respect my folks used to tell me I was rather like my great-grandmother, Esther Gregorie. At any rate, it was all fun. And I think that is what loving God is all about.

When my husband died a good many years ago, and when many of my good friends have preceded me in death, it has been very difficult. I have wept buckets of tears. But I never despaired. I never lost hope. For the presence of Christ in my life has filled me with the assurance that the purpose of life is not death but RESURRECTION. I believe in the resurrection of the dead—that God's love is so strong, so real, that he will be faithful even if I should lose faith.

And now, I have not much time left to me. The doctors say I have already lived longer than they expected. I do not want to die; I love living. But I'm not afraid. For I know that as God's love has sustained me throughout my ninety years, His love will continue to do so always. For this I am grateful.

Your parents and grandparents got me started—there at All Saints' Church in Fort Lauderdale. God bless them. I hope they know how much I appreciate what they did. I shall see them soon. I know I will.

And God bless you, too. Keep up the work of nurturing people in the faith.

Gratefully,

Mrs. Jonathan T. Jones
(Elizabeth Gregorie Shevock)

Preached by the Reverend Joseph M. Stoudenmire
February 19, 1989

Spring, 1999

"If you want to be proud of yourself, you've got to do things you can be proud of."

Words of Mrs. McCarty, a black woman who dropped out of school at 6th grade. She took in washing and did ironing for her entire working life, saving over two hundred and fifty thousand dollars. She gave her money to be used for college scholarships and was given presidential recognition by President Clinton.

Summer, 1999

"Sit steady in the boat."

The above was a favorite comment of George Hamlet Tatum, grandfather of my husband, William Hamlet Smith (Bill).

September 1999

"It would be well for all to remember that suspicion is far more apt to be wrong than right, and unfair and unjust than fair. It is a first cousin to prejudice and persecution and an unhealthy weed that grows with them."

Dr. Francis J. Braceland and Michael Stock, O. P.
April 2000

"After studying numerous patients, these authors saw a similarity among those who improved their lives despite many, varied, and often crushing circumstances, including the following:

* not dwelling on the past and damage done

* not blaming parents for what was less than desirable in them

* by not falling into the trap of calling themselves victims—taking that bait that others sometimes encourage (even though unintentional) by offering too much sympathy.

* found and built on their own strengths

* improved deliberately on their parents' lifestyle

* married consciously into strong, healthy families

* fought off memories of horrible get-togethers of family in order to establish regular mealtime routines, vacations and family celebrations and rituals of their own

"The authors stated that they learned competent families settled problems in this manner:

* defined the difficulty

* accepted problems as part of a normal life—not the result of a stigma or a punishment or weakness

* came together for a solution—stayed away from the "silent treatment" or the "yell and scream" approach and parents were given the leadership role, but allowed others to express ideas"

From the book *The Resilient Self*
April 2000

"When Henry James, of all people, was saying goodbye once to his young nephew, Billy, his brother, William's son, he said something that the boy never forgot. And of all the labyrinthine and impenetrable subtle things that most labyrinthine and impenetrable old romancer could have said, what he did say was this: 'There are three things that are important in human life. The first is to be kind. The second is to be kind. The third is to be kind.'"

From *Listening to Your Life* by Frederick Buechner
April 2000

"Let nothing disturb you; all things are passing. God never changes. Patience obtains all things. Nothing is wanting to him who possesses God. God alone suffices."

St. Theresa's Bookmark, FN 2-53
Quote given to Bill by Dr. Erdman
April 2000

A thing of beauty is a joy forever.

From the poem "Endymion" by John Keats

Beauty is truth . . . truth, beauty. That is all ye know on earth and all ye need to know.

From "Ode on a Grecian Urn" by John Keats

"Wisdom is the principle thing; therefore get wisdom and with all thy getting, get understanding."

Proverbs 4:7

This scripture quote appears above the entrance to Converse College Library, Spartanburg South Carolina

May 2000

"If man succeeds in removing suffering with pills and drops, then he will completely ignore religion and philosophy, in which he has so far found not only help against all affliction, but even happiness."

A. Chekov
May 28, 2002

There are exceptions to this when medications would be helpful.

R. T. S.

"[Thomas] Jefferson had impressive talents for diplomacy. He was cool, adroit, supple, resourceful, and patient. He approved (Ben) Franklin's rule . . . 'Never contradict anybody.' A disputant, he said, never wins an argument, but only widens the gap of disagreement. So it is much better to tolerate differences, insinuate doubts, ask questions, and in this good-humored fashion discover workable grounds of cooperation."

From *Thomas Jefferson and the New Nation*
by Merrill D. Peterson, page 388.

July 2003

Made in the USA
Columbia, SC
26 September 2020